David Del Tredici
'Cello Acrostic

BOOSEY & HAWKES

DISTRIBUTED BY

HAL•LEONARD®
CORPORATION
7777 W. BLUEMOUND RD. P.O. BOX 13819 MILWAUKEE, WI 53213

www.boosey.com
www.halleonard.com

Published by Boosey & Hawkes, Inc.
35 East 21st Street
New York NY 10010

www.boosey.com

ISMN 979-0-051-10558-8

First printed 2009

Printed in U.S.A. and distributed by Hal Leonard Corporation, Milwaukee WI

Music engraving by Peter Simcich

First performed February 14, 1998 at the
University of South Florida Music Recital Hall, Tampa
by Scott Kluksdahl, violoncello

PROGRAM NOTE

Pulitzer Prize-winning composer David Del Tredici's *Final Alice* is the fifth of six large works for soprano and orchestra based on Lewis Carroll's *Alice in Wonderland* books. It was commissioned in honor of the United States Bicentennial and was premiered by soprano Barbara Hendricks and the Chicago Symphony Orchestra under Sir Georg Solti in 1976. A subsequent recording by the same artists was issued on the Decca label.

'Cello Acrostic* is an arrangement of *Acrostic Song*, the lullaby-like concluding aria from *Final Alice*. The text is the seven-verse epilogue poem to *Through the Looking Glass*, the second of Lewis Carroll's *Alice* books. The poem is an acrostic: the initial letters of the lines spell out Alice Pleasance Liddell, the name of the real-life Alice for whom Carroll wrote his stories.

Duration: *ca.* 6 minutes

for Scott Kluksdahl

'CELLO ACROSTIC

arrangement of "Acrostic Song"

from *Final Alice*

Edited by Scott Kluksdahl

DAVID DEL TREDICI

Arranged by the composer

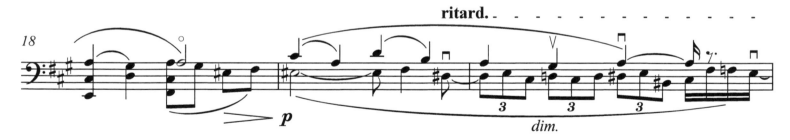

4

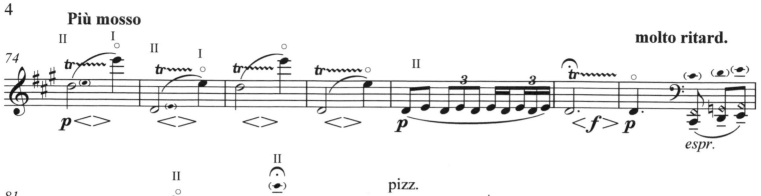

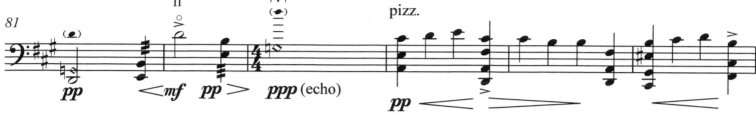

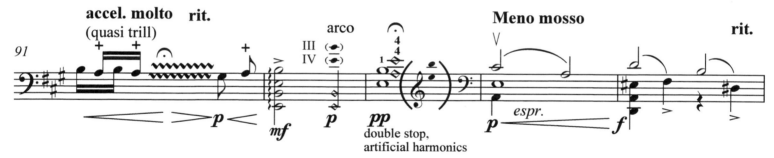

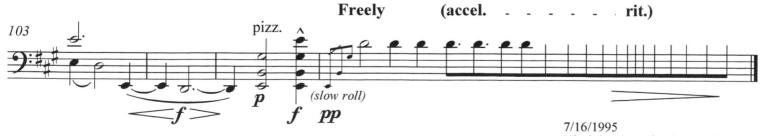

7/16/1995
Virginia Center for the Creative Arts